GROWN-UPS AND OTHER PROBLEMS

GROWN-UPS AND OTHER PROBLEMS

HELP FOR SMALL PEOPLE IN A BIG WORLD
BY PETER MAYLE & ARTHUR ROBINS

MACMILLAN PUBLISHING CO., INC. New York

Designed by Maggie Lewis

Library of Congress cataloging number 82-6523

ISBN 0-02-582550-X

Macmillan Publishing Co., Inc.
866 Third Avenue, New York, N.Y. 10022

Printed in Hong Kong

10   9   8   7   6   5   4   3   2   1

WORST THINGS FIRST: SCHOOL

Sooner or later, someone is going to tell you that your schooldays are the happiest days of your life. This is likely to make you miserable for weeks. After all, if school is the happiest time of your life, what is there to look forward to?

Cheer up. They are <u>not</u> the happiest days of your life. They are sometimes quite awful, because you suddenly have to cope with all kinds of problems on your own.

We asked some friends of ours what worries them most about going to school, and this is what they told us.

BULLIES

Most schools have one or two bullies. The best way to deal with them (if they're not too big and you're feeling brave) is to hit them back. Bullies are usually

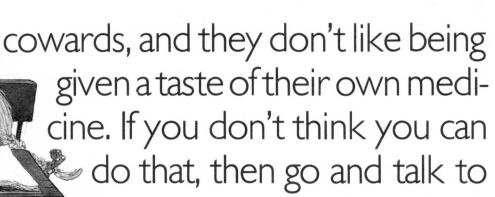

cowards, and they don't like being given a taste of their own medicine. If you don't think you can do that, then go and talk to your teacher. Teachers don't like bullies any more than you do.

SCHOOL FOOD

School food is famous for being terrible. It's as though the cooks have been specially taught to put lumps in the pudding, caterpillars in the lettuce, and what look like old toenails in the hamburger. Once in a while they make a mistake and cook something rather good, but most days it's pretty nasty. Our advice is to stick to home cooking, and take lunch with you in your biggest pocket.

EXAMINATIONS

It won't take you long to find out that there are

two kinds of people in the world: those who are good at exams, and those who go blank. If you're one of the blank brigade, there's not much you can do about it except try to relax; it's being nervous that makes you forget what you know.

BEING LAST

Someone always has to be last, whether it's in class or in sports. One day, unless you're very lucky, that someone is going to be you. It's nothing to be ashamed about, as long as you've done your best. Don't worry about it. You can't be good at everything.

LOSING YOUR BOOKS

It happens to all of us. School books have a way of getting left on the bus, dropped in the playground, or lost in a friend's house. The quickest way of getting them back is to write your name clearly in each book, and offer a reward of two comics, one white mouse and a chocolate bar to whoever finds them.

LOSING YOUR MOTHER

This is a bad moment indeed. There you are, waiting to be picked up from school, but nobody comes to collect you. Your mother has vanished. Your friends have all gone home. What are you to do? Grab the nearest teacher, and explain what's happened. Teachers are experts at finding missing mothers.

BEHIND THE EARS AND UNDER THE ARMS

What is the point of washing yourself and cleaning your teeth when you know very well they're only going to get dirty again?

And why does it have to be done every day? Why not a weekly wash? Or once a month? Or every other year? Who cares if there's a dollop of yesterday's breakfast on your chin and mushrooms growing out of your socks?

If you lived all alone on a desert island, maybe it wouldn't matter if you didn't have a bath from one year to the next. There would be nobody to see you (or smell you) except yourself.

But the world's a crowded place. You spend at home, on the bus, at school, at the movies. Imagine at home, on the bus, at school, in the cinema. Imagine what it would be like if you had to hold your nose every time someone else sat next to you. Worse still, imagine what it would be like if other people had to hold their noses when you sat next to them.

Everybody knows that washing and hav- ing baths isn't any fun. There's nothing much you can do in a bath except slosh around with the soap, and that

always seems to get in your eyes. So what's to be done?

The fastest way to get the whole thing over with is to have a shower instead of a bath. You get just as clean in half the time. But even a bath can be livened up if you wear a pair of frogmen's goggles. They're good at keeping the soap out of your eyes (specially when you're washing your hair), and you can do a bit of underwater exploring, practise holding your breath, and listen to all kinds of gurgling noises which you never hear with your head above water. Ask your mother to be the lifeguard until you've done it a few times.

Before you leave the bathroom, don't forget your teeth. Next to not washing, one of the easiest things in the world is not brushing your teeth. After all, they're not going to fall out if you sometimes forget to clean them.

That's true enough. But the trouble starts when you keep forgetting, or just don't bother. Dirty teeth

turn into decayed teeth. Decayed teeth give you toothache, and have to be taken out. Then you have to wear false teeth, which are uncomfortable and often make funny clicking noises when you're eating.

We're not making this up, and it's not something

that only happens to a few people. Half the grown-ups in Britain have to wear false teeth. Most of them would still have their own teeth today if they had only used their toothbrushes more often.

Until they make chocolate flavored toothpaste, you probably won't enjoy brushing your teeth. But you might like to try an electric toothbrush. It really tingles, and it does a grand job of cleaning those tricky bits round the back.

THE GREAT BEDTIME BATTLE

Grown-ups are tricky to deal with when it comes to bedtime. They always want you to go to bed when you want to stay up, and stay in bed when you want to get up. They themselves stay up so late you'd think they never want to go to bed; and once in bed, they want to stay there for as long as possible in the morning.

When it comes to your bedtime arrangements, the rules change. You are packed off to bed several hours before anyone else, and long before you feel sleepy. The idea is that you should get a Good Night's Sleep Because You're Growing.

There's no doubt that you need sleep. But do you need as much sleep as they think you need? Or is there some other reason why you hardly have time to finish your tea before they want to tuck you in?

Yes, there is. It's something that they will probably describe to you as "a little peace and quiet." All this means is that they want to spend some time reading the paper, watching TV, talking about the neighbours or generally not having to keep an eye on you.

The secret here is to <u>give</u> them a little peace and quiet. The quieter and more peaceful you are, the better your chances of staying up. Being almost invisible helps too, so if you can find an out of the way spot like under the dining table or behind the couch, your chances are even better.

There is a snag: sitting very still and keeping very quiet is so boring that you might make the terrible mistake of falling asleep. Then they've got you. It all depends

on how good you are at being quiet without getting bored.

The rules change yet again at the weekend. For six days a week you're supposed to get up early. On Sunday you're supposed to stay in bed late. This is the only morning of the week when your parents can have that extra couple of hours in bed that they always seem to want. (It's not surprising they're tired when you think how late they go to bed.) If you disturb this Sunday morning snooze, there will be black looks and threats about pocket money.

It's not that they mind you getting up, as long as you don't make <u>them</u> get up. So you have the whole of the house to yourself. This makes Sunday morning the perfect time to hold frog races in the bath, play hide-and-seek with the guinea pig in the linen closet, or eat chocolate biscuits. As long as you eat them quietly.

HOW TO ASK

It's worth practising your asking until you're an expert at it. People who know how to ask get what they want more often than people who don't.

This is true whether you're talking to grown-ups or other children, and whether you're asking for more ice cream or an elephant for Christmas.

Asking isn't easy. Not only do you have to ask in the right way, but you have to ask at the right time. For instance, it's no good asking your father for anything on a wet weekday morning when he's already late for work. As a rule, you should try to avoid asking your parents for <u>anything</u> during the week. They're always busy. This makes them forget what it was they said yes to, and then you have to start all over again.

Pick your moment during the weekend. Fathers are normally at their most good-tempered on Sunday

mornings. Mothers are better on Saturday nights. Don't ask us why. It varies from person to person, but you'll soon work out when your particular grown-ups are usually in a good mood, and that's the time to pounce.

Now we come to the business of exactly how to ask. This depends on what it is you're asking for – a second helping at lunchtime doesn't need the same amount of cunning as a trip to the zoo. But whatever it is you want, there are four words you should never use.

They are "I want" and "Give me". The reason you shouldn't use them is that they're very easy to say no to. And the secret of successful asking is to get a yes.

Here are a few examples which might come in handy.

"I'm feeling quite faint. Do you think I could have a chocolate ice cream?"

(This works for any flavor, and for drinks as well.)

"You don't mind if I stay up a little later, do you? I must finish this film script."

"I think you could do with a treat. Why don't I take you to the circus?"

"My friend seems to have lost his trousers. Is it all right if he stays the night?"

"I used to think an alligator would be a good pet, but I think you'd be happier with ferrets, wouldn't you?"

As you see, these are not just plain old boring demands. They're almost little stories. And there's a reason in each one why the answer should be yes.

Grown-ups love reasons. And, although it doesn't always seem that way, they like to say yes. All you have to do is make it as easy for them as you can.

'STOP THE WORLD! I WANT TO THROW UP!'

We all feel sick sometimes. The older you get, the easier it is to cope with because you get better at knowing when it's going to happen. When you're young, it somehow creeps up on you and catches you by surprise.

The worst thing you can do is to keep quiet about it until the very last moment. By then, it's too late for people around you to do anything except get out of the way. But if you can give them a couple of minutes warning, they might be able to do something to help— even if it's just to point you in the right direction.

You can also help yourself. If you know that eating bananas dipped in lemonade powder while you're riding on the bus makes you feel sick, don't do it.

If reading in the car makes you feel sick (and it affects a lot of people that way), then don't read.

If you get seasick in the bath, take a shower instead.

If flying makes you feel sick, make sure you have one of those special airsick bags.

If you can, it's best to avoid doing what you think will make you sick. If that's not possible (like the times when you have to fly), the next best thing is to plan for the worst. Take a travel sickness tablet, tuck a sickbag in your pocket, and sit where you can get some air. When you know you've done all you can, chances are that you'll be able to relax.

And since worry and nerves cause you to throw up just as often as eating too much, if you're relaxed you probably won't be sick.

Remember that nobody is going to get cross with you for feeling sick as long as you tell them. People only get upset when you're suddenly sick over their best shoes, their car, or their favorite cat.

GERBILS, WHITE MICE AND YOUR MOTHER

You will find that grown-ups in general and your mother in particular do not share your love of pets. (Specially pets which slither, eat furniture or have babies under the bed.)

Mothers see pets only as things that cause more mess and therefore more work. When you say that you'd like a pet, mothers say: "Who's going to look after it?"

They know the answer. <u>They're</u> going to look after it. So when you're deciding on a pet, remember that the less trouble it is to look after, the more likely you are to get it. Here are a few suggestions.

<u>STUFFED OWL</u> A favorite with mothers everywhere, since he needs very little looking after apart from dusting. Not much fun, though. And unless you turn its face to the corner, you'll find its eyes follow you round the room.

<u>GRASS SNAKES</u> are friendly creatures (they wag their tails) who go to sleep for several months each year. One grass snake we knew fell asleep in a shirt pocket and was put in the washing machine with the shirt. He shrunk to the size of a small worm.

<u>TORTOISE</u> It eats very little, and doesn't often smile. Bad on walks, unless you like walks that last for two or three days. The worst thing you can do to a

tortoise is turn it on its back. It hates you seeing its wrinkled underpants.

   FISH are interesting to watch but difficult to cuddle. They don't need much looking after, apart from special fish food. Feeding them on old cheese sand-wiches gives them wind.

   FROGS are good pets to have if you want to keep grown-ups out of your bedroom. All it takes is a

notice on the door which says BEWARE OF THE FROG.

GERBILS are not popular with mothers because they eat almost anything. Gerbils have been known to eat half a pair of trousers and a small sweater in one sitting.

MICE always seem to come in pairs. They need to be watched

carefully, because they are likely to have babies when you're not looking. Do not let them go into the linen closet.

<u>CATS</u> will put up with you as long as you do what they want. If you upset them, watch out. They will bring something nasty in from the garden and leave it on your bed.

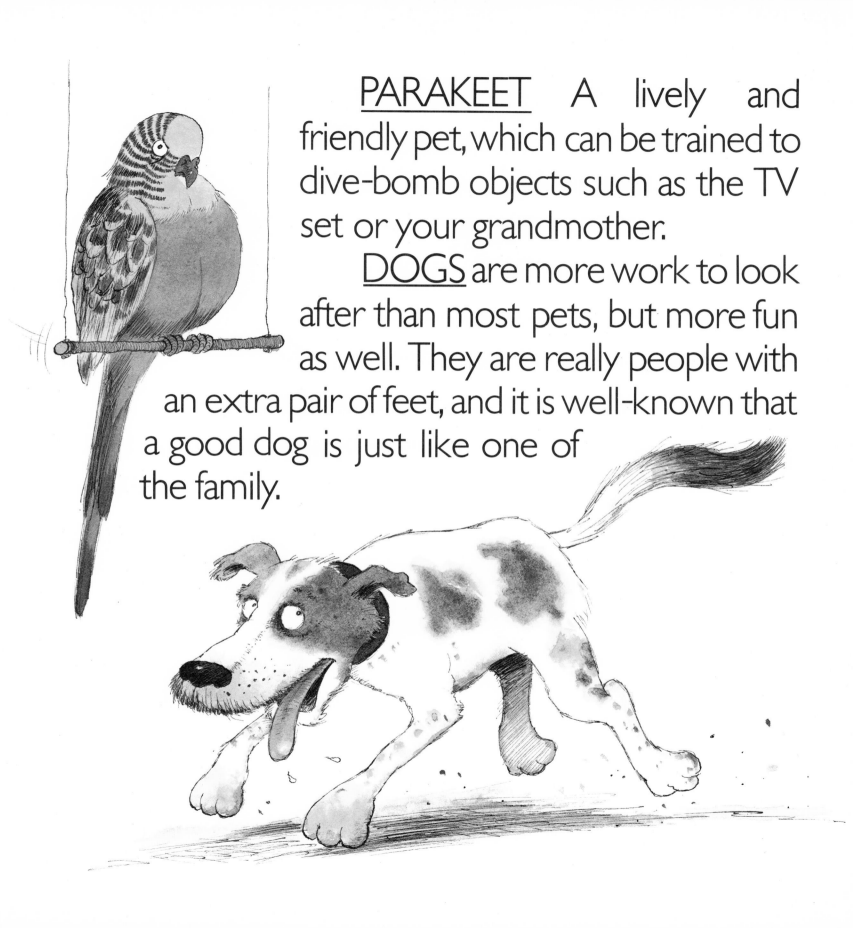

<u>PARAKEET</u> A lively and friendly pet, which can be trained to dive-bomb objects such as the TV set or your grandmother.

<u>DOGS</u> are more work to look after than most pets, but more fun as well. They are really people with an extra pair of feet, and it is well-known that a good dog is just like one of the family.

THE OPPOSITE SEX

In the animal kingdom there are certain species that don't get on with each other. Cats and dogs. Foxes and chickens. Sharks and almost anything. Birds and worms.

They are natural enemies, and whenever they meet there's trouble.

Most people would add girls and boys to that list.

For many years, the opposite sex is a pest. As you get older, the situation gets better, but what do you do in the meantime?

There are two specially difficult problems. The first is when your mother tries to make you become friends with the person of the opposite sex who lives next door.

The only answer is a heart-to-heart talk with your mother. Tell her that you'd rather make friends

with a rattlesnake than that little horror. Tell her you'll scrub floors, wash dishes, clean shoes – <u>anything</u> as long as you don't have to go next door for the afternoon. With a bit of luck, your mother will take the hint.

The other problem is when one of Them keeps following you around and wanting to join in whatever you're doing.

You can always try simple scare tactics:

"I have Athlete's Foot, and it's very catching."
or
"I think I'm going to be sick."
If those don't work, you'll have to try more serious stuff. Here are some ideas:

TO GET RID OF A BOY
Ask him to be the nurse when you play doctors and nurses.
Give him your doll to carry.
Threaten to kiss him.

TO GET RID OF A GIRL
Always have something horrible in your pocket.
Ask her to hold your pet cockroach while you play football.
Introduce her to your smelliest friend.

THE TERRORS OF THE TABLE

There are thousands of things you can eat. There are hundreds of ways of cooking them. But there are only three kinds of food.

1. Food that you like.
2. Food you're not sure about.
3. Food that makes you feel sick.

The first kind is the food you eat at home, and on birthdays. No difficulties there.

The second kind can give you some nasty moments. Not because of the food itself, but because it's always given to you when you're away from home. This can make even the most friendly plate of baked beans on toast look different and slightly suspicious.

When you're not sure about what's being dished

up, it's best to ask for a small helping. You can't leave a huge plateful untouched and hope nobody will notice. But a small helping can be divided into even smaller blobs and left around the plate until it looks as though you've eaten most of it. If, to your surprise, you find that you actually like it, you can ask for more. Cooks are always pleased if you like their cooking.

It's the third kind of food that causes the most trouble. For us, it was always tapioca pudding (the stuff that looks like frogspawn), liver with tubes in it, or salad, which we were sure was infested with slugs. For you, it could be anything from macaroni cheese to pork chops. There are bound to be one or two things which make your heart sink as you see them coming towards you on the plate. You know that one mouthful – even without swallowing – will make you sick.

You can either sit there and drink umpteen glasses of water while the Thing on your plate gets cold

and even more disgusting. Or you can do this: just say, "I'm very sorry, but liver (or whatever it is) doesn't agree with me."

This is a pleasant and polite way of saying no. Any sensible person will leave it at that, and not ask you to force down a couple of mouthfuls. People who do insist have only themselves to blame for what happens next.

AWAY FROM HOME

Staying the night at a friend's house is one of life's little pleasures. Parents are usually on their best behaviour. Bedtime is later than usual, and bathtime is often forgotten altogether. All in all, it's like a short holiday.

But because it's away from home, you must be prepared for everything to be different. For instance:

FOOD

Other mothers' cooking is not always as tasty as the food you get at home. If you're not sure about what you're going to be given to eat, pack a few titbits in with your pyjamas.

NOISES AT NIGHT

All houses have their own special set of night-time noises. You get so used to the sounds in your own house that you don't even notice them. But the minute

you turn out the light in a strange room, you start hearing things. Crocodiles in the water pipes! Burglars under the bed! Giant toads outside the window! Snakes! Wolves! Help!

Put the light on, and they go away. Keep the light on, and they stay away.

THE VANISHING LOO

You know the way to the bathroom at home with your eyes closed, which is just as well when you need to go in the middle of the night. But where exactly is the bathroom in your friend's house? Could you find it in the dark? Are you sure? Goodness knows where you might end up if you're not certain of your geography.

OTHER PEOPLE'S PETS

One young friend of ours had a nasty shock when she was bitten by what she thought was a black rug. She stepped on it, and it turned into a dog. There

are other stories of people being attacked by parrots they thought were stuffed, cats they thought were asleep, and hedgehogs that were supposed to be hibernating. The moral of these stories is: don't touch other people's pets unless you've been properly introduced.

OTHER PEOPLE'S PARENTS

They will always give you the benefit of the doubt the first time you do something awful. After that, they'll simply send you home. So you should treat them more care-fully than your own parents until you get to know their little ways.

MONEY

Money is great fun when you have some, and a problem when you haven't. It is almost always a problem for grown-ups.

Without being asked, they will tell you how diffi-cult money is to find, and where it <u>doesn't</u> come from. (It doesn't grow on trees, your father isn't made of it, and so on.)

Well, where <u>does</u> it come from? And how can you make sure that some of it comes your way?

The nearest sources of money are your parents. They get it by working for it, and they probably give you a little each week to buy vital supplies like ice cream and comics. But for real money - the kind that buys bicycles

– you can't expect them to pay up without giving them a nudge in the right direction.

For example, serious collectors of money never have birthday or Christmas presents. They have money instead. Not very exciting, but it's a good steady income.

Or, of course, you can make some money the way your parents do, by working for it. Have a look around the house, and you'll find dozens of jobs that grown-ups hate, and would pay you to do.

You must be careful, though. The scale of charges has to be agreed before you start, or you'll spend all your time arguing about payment.

One sound and businesslike way of doing this is to have a list of jobs and agree prices for each with the management (your mother). For something quick and easy, like laying the table, your price will obviously be low. Bigger jobs, like washing the car, will pay bigger prices. Jobs that are specially difficult or dangerous, like giving the cat a bath, will have to be worked out separately.

Here are half a dozen little jobs that most grown-ups will go to almost any lengths (even paying money) to avoid.

* Cleaning shoes properly. (Use of spit forbidden.)
* Walking the dog.
* Getting rid of the ring in the bath tub.
* Washing up after Sunday lunch.
* Weeding, mowing the lawn, or digging.
* Changing the tray in the bird's cage.

One last tip. Always ask for payment in advance. You never know your luck.

OUCH! HOSPITALS, DOCTORS AND DENTISTS

Most people, no matter how old and brave they are, feel nervous about visiting the doctor or spending half an hour in the dentist's chair. And nobody actually enjoys going into hospital.

It's a shame we all feel like this, because hospitals, doctors and dentists are there to help us. The trouble is that when we need them, we're feeling ill or in pain. Afterwards, when we think of the doctor or the dentist we remember that it hurt when we saw them. That makes us nervous about seeing them again.

Another reason for feeling nervous is the strangeness of everything – specially in a hospital. The rooms are bigger, the beds are different, the smell is different, the food tastes different. Even hospital pyjamas aren't like the ones you wear at home. There are big

and rather scary machines all over the place too. Faced with all this and feeling ill as well, it's no wonder we don't

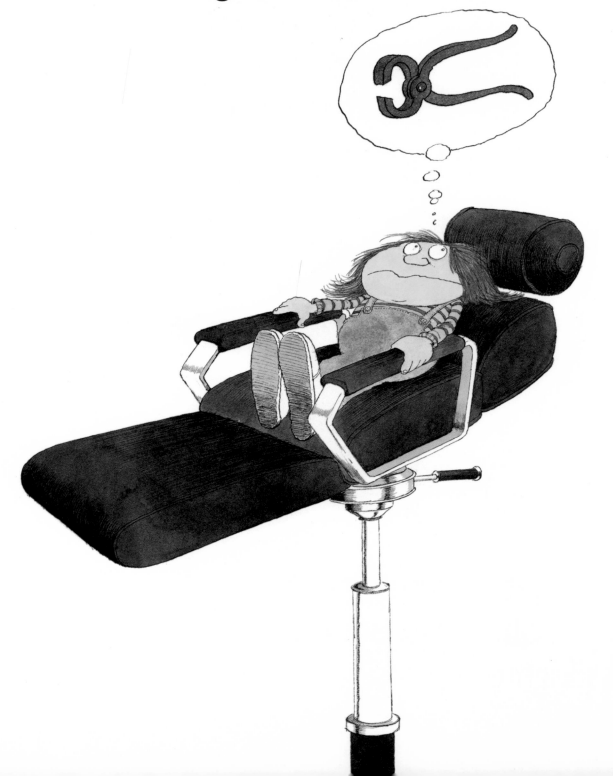

enjoy the idea of a few days in hospital.

And yet nearly all of us go into hospital at some time in our lives. About half the children in this country have been to hospital by the time they're seven years old. And we all need to visit the doctor and dentist from time to time.

There's not a lot you can do to stop yourself feeling ill. But there is a way to make those visits less frightening.

It's very simple. Just ask your parents to take you along to the doctor, or the dentist, or the hospital one day. Not to have anything done, but to have a look. You'll find that the people are friendly and that those machines are there to help you get better when you're ill.

Hospital will never be a place where you want to spend your holidays. But the more you know about it, the less frightening it is.

SECRET WEAPONS

There are certain times during the year (birthdays, Christmas, the week before your school report arrives) when you might like to be on specially good terms with your grown-ups.

This is not as easy as you think. It isn't enough just to be your normal charming and well-behaved self – that's taken for granted. No, you need to do something so unusual and wonderful that it gets noticed.

How can you tell that it _has_ been noticed? By the reaction of your grown-ups. They will first of all be pleased. Very quickly after that they will want to know what you're up to. Sometimes they will even ask you what you want.

Don't tell them, or you'll spoil the effect of what you've done. Smile, say nothing and let them work it out for themselves.

Exactly what you have to do to make this happen will vary from one grown-up to another. If you think about it hard, you'll invent a few secret weapons of your own. Meanwhile, here are three little winners that always used to work for us.

BREAKFAST IN BED

This may seem to you like a messy way to start the day, but grown-ups love it. There's no need to do anything as complicated as the full egg-and-bacon breakfast. In fact, it's much better not to. Fried eggs have a nasty habit of sliding off the plate and into the bed. Tea or coffee and toast is perfect. It's not actually what they eat that matters to grown-ups as much as not having to get up to eat it. Strange but true.

PEACE AND QUIET

You can wash behind your ears every night for six months, but it won't work as well as thirty minutes of peace and quiet. Sunday morning is without doubt the best time of the week for this, and if you want to go for total victory, you can combine peace and quiet and breakfast in bed. If that doesn't work, nothing will. But be careful you don't overdo it, or they'll expect it every weekend.

OWNING UP

If you have done something truly bad, don't wait

until it's found out; that only makes it worse. Take a deep breath, pick the grown-up who seems to be in the best mood, and tell all. It's not easy, but it usually works. And in the end, it's more comfortable than running away to sea.